Genre Fantasy

MW00592940

Essential Question
How do friends depend on each other?

by Jacqui Briggs

illustrated by Chris Vallo

Cass loved her home. She played with Ricky.

She slept in the yard. She
did what she wanted.

Dibs ran across the yard.
A new home! He looked
around.

"Look! A big yard!" Dibs
barked. He ran. He played.
His actions were happy.

"Hi," said Kathy. "This is my dog, Dibs."

"Hi," said Ricky nervously. Would he need to rescue Dibs from Cass? She hated dogs.

"Kathy, do you like swings?" asked Ricky. "I do!"

"Let's play on the swings!" said Kathy.

"Let's play, Cat!" barked Dibs.

Cass peered at Dibs. "My name is Cass. I don't like dogs," she meowed.

"I know a game. I can show you," barked Dibs.

"I don't play with dogs," hissed Cass.

Dibs wagged his tail.

Dibs hit the ball. Cass hit it back. She didn't like dogs. But she forgot.

"You hit it perfectly," barked Dibs. "You're good at this game."

They were playing together!

"Yay! I like this ball game," meowed Cass.

"I'm afraid I'm getting tired," barked Dibs.

"I know a secret. I will show you," meowed Cass.

Dibs followed Cass under a bush. It was cool and dark. Dibs stretched out.

"What now?" Dibs barked.

"We nap," purred Cass.

"Our pets made friends,"
said Ricky.

"I'm glad," said Kathy.

"Can we be friends, too?"
asked Ricky.

"Yes. You can depend on
me," said Kathy.

Respond to Reading

Summarize

Use details to summarize *Cat and Dog.*

Detail	Detail	Detail

Text Evidence

1. How do you know *Cat and Dog* is a fantasy story? Genre

2. What does Cass like to play? Use story details. Key Details

3. Use your knowledge of inflectional endings to figure out what *playing* means on page 10. Inflectional Endings

4. Write about how Cass and Dibs met. Use details to help you. Write About Reading

Compare Texts
Read about a squirrel and his uncle who depend on each other.

Uncle Max and I

When I was a baby,
my Uncle Max
played with me
and gave me snacks.

As I got older,
he taught me the facts:
Where to find acorns,
and how to read tracks.

Now he is old.
Together we relax.
There's no better pal
than my Uncle Max.

Make Connections

How do the squirrels depend on each other? Essential Question

How are they like the neighbors in *Cat and Dog*? Text to Text

Focus on Genre

Fantasy A fantasy story is a story that could not happen in real life. The characters in the story may seem real. But they have special powers.

What to Look for The animals in *Cat and Dog* can talk. Real animals cannot talk.

Your Turn

Create your own fantasy characters. What special powers do they have? Draw a picture of your characters trying out their special powers.